You're  This? My Ramblings on Social Media

Jason Pollock

Gene,
I hope this enhances your bathroom time!

J. Pollock

Holy crap.. Turn the page.

DEDICATION

This book goes out to my always supportive wife, Laura.
I hope this helps us get caught up on the mortgage.

This is the best photobomb that ever happened to me. Erin Moran (Joanie from Happy Days for you younger folks) was apparently shocked at my posing for this picture. I had no idea she was there.

CONTENTS

I sent this picture to my now wife when I was courting her. She still went for it. That makes her a keeper.

ACKNOWLEDGMENTS

I also want to thank Josh, Judah, Mark, Will Bozarth, Joe Knetter, Kegan Lusk, Lori Longstreath, mom-in-law, mom, dad, Heather, Sophia, Joey, Chris.. and so on.. for inspiring me to get this done. Along with every single one of my Facebook friends. I wish there were too many to mention by name. There are, but not quite at that 5000 mark. Still too many to write on here.

Not meaning to show off, but I did meet a muppet. Proud moment.

Hello Reader! First of all, I just want to thank you for purchasing the first book I ever wrote. You might like it. You might not. You're still in the early stages of reading it. You'll really find out as you go.

Let me tell you a little bit about who I am before you really start to question, "Who is this person and why should I care about him?" That's a very good question. You don't need to care. I'm really nobody special or just as significant as any other human. This is just a project I wanted to work on and actually complete. On the celebrity scale from A-List to D-List celebrities, I'm around a T-Lister; not quite at the end of the alphabet. I'm a comedian/actor. Granted, I'm not what you would call a successful comedian/actor, in part due to a certain degree of laziness. I was the gm of a now defunct club called Rascals Comedy Club in Cherry Hill, NJ till June of 2007. Since then, I've lived lifetimes. Different jobs through temp agencies, retail, accounting assistant, comedy club booker, and some cool performing gigs.

In 2011, I got married to a woman I started dating a year prior. It just worked. Now, I could audition more, but the thought of being home with her and collecting a steady paycheck is really comforting and safe. This book is an attempt to break out of my safe zone and get back into having a creative mind again whilst still spending time with the love of my life.

Thanks to social media, we've all kind of been writing as long as we've been on it; a modern day diary, if you will. After talking to a writer friend about wanting to accomplish SOMETHING, he told me that he did a book very similar and said I should do it too. I told him that was his idea and I can't. He didn't give a crap. Having said that, I made mine. I can't take credit for having an idea for writing a book solely based on my Facebook and Twitter statuses. However, I can say that it's based on MY Facebook and Twitter. Some references might be dated and before I was married. Others are somewhat up to date. The longer you hold onto this however, the more in the past the references get. It doesn't automatically update. If you like it, just find me on social media. If not, sorry. Thanks for buying.

Please enjoy.

1 RANDOM THOUGHTS

This is the random section. This section is filled with random statuses with very little to no connection to one another. I figured I'd put the random chapter in the front of the book before the specific chapters. If I put it at the end, you might say to yourself, "He had chapters that seemed organized, but then he just gave up and threw everything into a random chapter." NOW, you can say, "It started out really random. THEN, he got his shit together."

(My First Facebook Comment from a former Starbucks barista! That's where introverts would meet girls.)
November 16, 2007
HEYYYYY!!! I am the Very first person to write on your wall and I am very excited about that!!!

I'm updating my status to something wonderful that will make all your dreams come true. Look! A magic squirrel.

When will they release the complete Larry Ferrari series on dvd?

I haven't updated my status for a while. I am out of thoughts.

What's a concert without salmon?

One day someone will create the greatest status update EVER!

I wore his Neil Diamond concert shirt to the gym and still no girls talked to me.

My dentist is coming in at 11 tomorrow morning (Sunday) to fix the tooth issue. Should I tip or bring wine? What do you do in that situation? Do you just say thanks?

I'm not going to shower or shave on Earth Day this morning in an attempt to conserve water and really just sleep later. Today, I am a dirty hippie.

Buses are awkward.

I'm watching Tyler Perry's Schindler's List.

Yep.. I remember the Alamo.

I'm using goats to mow my lawn. They are all gathered in one place! How do you guys get them to move around so the lawn is even?!

I just realized I have no friends named Abner! Dammit!

I wish I could sell my body fat for cash.

I saw 3 giraffes at work today. I normally don't see 1. Today I saw 3. Well, it is Friday.

My point is that people need to see things from all perspectives and admit when they are wrong.

How many women find dudes playing air instruments hot?

A man I just met, started a story by saying, "I was running down this alley in North Philly barefoot... " as an example of a story about how he was afraid of bugs. He didn't acknowledge why! I have to accept that he just runs down alleys in bad neighborhoods barefoot.

I just saw a little kid whack his mom in the head with the divider stick at the register in Shop Rite. Made my day!

I actually saw a chicken today trying to cross the street. I can't figure out why he would do that.

I accidentally ate a smurf. I thought it was a marshmallow.

I'm driving through Camden, NJ. One hand on the wheel. Windows down. Dolly Parton's 9 to 5 is blaring out of the windows. I am badass.

I have a tradition of putting a little bit of coffee on my shirt and pants every morning while I'm driving. I believe it's good luck.

I will be living in Philadelphia for a little bit after next week. There's still, at least, another move after that. I am David Banner without the radiation, just a dude who moves a lot.

I'm dog and housesitting till Friday. I am hoping I don't change into the Hulk, for some reason. I need this house and the dogs to stay just as they left it. Please no gamma radiation here.

I had a dream last night that I was in a gas station explosion and I turned into the Incredible Hulk. Only I didn't grow in height and everyone was laughing at me and it hurt my self-esteem.

Well, I'm technically homeless till tomorrow. Bob Geldof? A little help?

Why do all the guys in the Lady Gaga's Alejandro video have the Moe haircut? Was this a weird fantasy of hers?

"They have edible mugs. They're called ice cream cones!" I heard this quote tonight from a very smart woman, believe it or not. I wanted to share. Pour your coffee into an ice cream cone and see what happens.

Sometimes when I sleep on my left side, my ear folds in a little and it really hurts when I wake up. I hate that. You know?

Jason Pollock
July 13, 2010
It's the 25th anniversary of Live Aid! It's been 25 years ago that world hunger was ended forever with great music.

(Mayan Calendar joke)
I just noticed that my car doesn't need to be inspected again till April of 2012. Does that mean I have gone through my last car inspection?

I got hold of the Mayan swimsuit calendar of 2012!

This is going to be a great week! No animals were harmed in the making of this update. Good morning!

Ball... rooms hahahaha!

Remember the days when a Who song was simply a Who song and not known as the theme to CSI.

I was at the bar at a comedy club and Yanni just came on the jukebox. What kind of a bar has Yanni on the jukebox?!

I'm still awake. Remember the days, in high school, when you're up at this hour trying to get hold of someone and it's busy so you use an emergency breakthrough?

I've never done it with Anne Hathaway, despite rumors.

Can aspirin cure Stockholm Syndrome?

(This is what people do on Facebook.)
I'm off to a relaxing Sunday afternoon bbq. Sorry. Nothing weird here. Just sayin what I'm doin.

I was skipping rocks with his friend, Josh. Josh told me that I can't skip rocks to save my life. When would I ever need to?

(Smart people get this reference)
I just found out all the dolphin's left! Oh no! Do you know what that means?

I'm sitting behind a couple at a diner who is having a casual break up argument. She is saying, "Stop dwelling on it." I admire her attitude.

Does making hives appear and disappear considered a superpower. I need tap into this and control it.

I'm having the 3rd moving day of the summer. I'm going to stay positive. I'm not a nomad. I'm a yesmad.

I do not remember ever eating Kix cereal.

For those of you who don't know, plastic shower caps, when dropped from a high floor window, look like flying jelly fish.

Do The Lockhorns ever age?

I had the best chicken, coffee, and Life cereal breakfast!

How do walruses mate? It just seems impossible!

(Yom Kippur)
Not only did I not fast today, but through a series of unfortunate circumstances, is eating Canadian bacon.

The writers of the tv show of my life have come up with some great new characters over the years and never seem to run out of ideas. It just gets exhausting to keep up with them.

I would love to drive a tank, but cannot conceive of when or how that would ever happen.

I'm on a train to NYC and heading to the New York Comedy Club. It would be so cool if this train went underwater and we saw things out the window.

I'm home after being awake for almost 24 hours again. I have a Meredith Baxter Burning desire for Sleep! Woohoo!

I just had a refreshing soul-cleansing sneeze. You know, the kind you feel throughout your whole body? I think I lost weight from that one!

I managed to use the term Life Burger in a sentence tonight. I am very proud of myself. Feel free to take that and use it yourself.

What is better for breakfast than a pretzel hot dog?! Nothing! Unless I have a fruit salad presented to me by laughing gnomes.

Laughter is not the best medicine for a sore throat and a cough.

I got new wiper blades today and I feel my car runs so much better.

(No idea what play this could've been)
It was a fun opening night. Thanks to those who came last night. Maybe tonight we can get some brave people to sit in the front two rows. We have ponchos, don't worry, because you will get wet.

Blackmail seems to be an easy way to make money. Anyone have anything personal they want to share?

What is the consensus? Is fire two syllables?

I would love to hear about interesting or famous people you rode with in an elevator.

I just saw a chicken trying to cross the road again. Why would he do that?

Does anyone else get confused at the difference between Anne Murray and Helen Reddy?

I wish there was value in dryer lint.

What's the difference in knowing what numbers are odd and what numbers are even. What difference does it make in our lives?

(No Idea.. Trying to sound intelligent)
I'm posting the pinnacle of a tautologial status! Right?! Thanks Chris!

Chris B. Technically, by explicitly calling it tautological you have posted a metatautological status, which makes your status false. But if you posted that you were posting a metatautological status, that would be a metametatautological status, and would thus still be false. The only way i think you could logically get away with this would be to post that you were posting a metatautological status, with a bar above the prefix meta, to indicate an unending string of meta-s. Or for added fun, you could post a status that reads "This status is false" Think about it...

What would you get Paul McCartney for his birthday?He can have anything he wants. I'm glad we're not friends.

I got 2 1/2 hours of sleep. One way to deal with that is to look at being awake as feeling like you are on legal narcotics

So one of the cats decided against the litter box and pooped on a small carpet. She then folded the carpet in half to hide it. They are smarter than they appear to be. Do not be fooled.

I've never said, "Gabe Kaplan! Get back here you!" for any reason and can't imagine when I would get that opportunity.

I would like to remind you all, as a public service, to check the toilet seat before sitting on it. At the park bathroom today, there was a tick just hanging out there waiting.

"Great murderers, like great men in other walks of activity, have blue eyes." - Anonymous

(Weird moment for Josh and myself)
Josh P
May 20, 2011
Hanging with Jason Pollock and Sherman Hemsley. Let the rapture begin!

I just saw two rabbits humping like... um... rabbits?

(Someone quoted me)
"You're not a vulgar talker....I mean....you're not a vulgarian." - Jason Pollock

If you are unsure of a word having one or two Ls in it, just double up to be safe. You can never have too many Ls. If you are truly confident, just go with one.

I am so anti-histimine.

Shapeshifter or the power to play any instrument and play perfectly without any experience? What would you choose? This is important stuff.

There is a difference between a tooth extract and vanilla extract. However, one can cause the other eventually.

Just an fyi... I saw an ice cream man run out of his truck into a port-a-potty. You know this man did not wash his hands. Be careful out there ice cream buyers.

I think shadows are the only form of nature's real life animation.

A pimple in the ear is not a comfortable Monday.

If people could suddenly fly, think of how bad the economy would become. The number of unemployed would sky rocket. Nobody would drive anymore!

One word: Pumpkin beer is awesome!

At approximately 9:00 this morning, my body realized that I ate two bowls of chili last night. It wanted to let me know.

A friend of mine posted a very poignant and topical question I wanted to share. Who would you rather do? Amanda Knox or Casey Anthony?

With the population out of control, we should eliminate all seat belt laws.

I had a wasp outside my car window. They were rolled up so I locked the door. That seemed like a rational decision at that moment. In retrospect, I don't know what that would accomplish.

Pandora just played me a song called I'm Saving My Hymen For Jesus. I don't know what else to say

I have a question. When a snake poops, does it get smeared on the rest of the remaining body past the snake butt?

Until about a year ago I always thought Roy Orbison was blind. Was I the only who thought that?

I have been coughing so hard it gave me a head rush. In your face people who pay good money for those! Ha!

Nothing rhymes with Bosom, does it.

I was just out for a walk and this kid walking towards me with his mom pointed and shouted, "Look mommy! A stranger!" First of all, he doesn't even know me. Secondly, he was a little too excited over it.

Would you read a self-help book entitled, "Living the Good Life with CamelToe?"

Jason Pollock
April 20, 2012
Happy birthday Hitler! We own everything now! In your face!

(An excited fan, dreaming)
"Wait was it a dream or is Jason Pollock getting a tattoo of my face on his chest????!!! Please be real life. Please be real life."

(A former employee of mine who does not believe in suing. Really, it's not what you think.)
"So I'm currently having sporatic back pains now due to the fact that u made me do 2 splits at work today. I should of stretched more. I curse u and these back pains!"

"What is a Japanese company doing making a game about an Italian plumber?!" - My friend's 5 year old son re: Super Mario

Is there an entry in the Guinness Book for the longest Excel spreadsheet?

If I were Dennis the Menace what would I put on Facebook? "I just peaked in The Wilson's bedroom window and saw their beds pushed together! Mr. Wilson, you're bad! SMH!"

So DC Comics made a gay superhero before a Jewish one. I guess it's because a Jewish superhero would have too many vices against it. They couldn't fight crime From Friday to Saturday night for one thing.

After standing in a long line at the Redbox, I thought, "What a great idea it would be to open an entire shop where people can come and rent these things without waiting one at a time to return and we'll have a bigger selection!" Any takers?

I feel fortunate, in a way, that if someone steals my identity, they'll be worse off then they were before. It would be even better if with identity theft, all your bills get transferred to them as well.

There is no way that my cats will ever know what a cell phone is. I'm getting anxious thinking that they'll never grasp this concept no matter how much I try to explain.

(Brilliant marketing to get people to performances)
I just got some ink on my hands from a pen. If you come to the Dark Horse tonight I'll show you exactly where, on the side of my hand, it stained before it disappears.

Geico is sending me letters reading, "Baby, Come Back" which is a little personal to call me Baby. Allstate's new ad is telling us they want to be our friend with benefits. It sounds like Geico is about the love and Allstate wants to use me. I'm afraid of what State Farm has to offer.

Sometimes there is too much responsibility being the son of Zeus. I need a drink.

I feel like since we are paying to drive on the New Jersey Turnpike, we shouldn't have to sit in traffic.

They might not have food in Ethiopia, but they can make a hell of a good coffee. Maybe if they didn't drink so much of it, they wouldn't be so hungry.

When cats dream can they get weird like people's? Would my cat be putting on shoes in his mind? Do you think they know it's just a dream?

To all my Mormon polygamist friends, there's got to be a least favorite wife. I refuse to believe that you're all loved equally.

(Also a misunderstanding)
Ashley
to
Jason Pollock
August 23, 2012 ·
I have rug burn on my elbows from last nights tripping lol

If I were a woman, I would think that if I found out I was pregnant, I would need a drink more than ever. AND YOU CAN'T DO IT! I have to give you moms credit. I don't know how you coped.

As far as the subject of chocolate and caramel covered apples go, they're not bad. Apples are really nature's toothbrush. After you eat through the chocolate and caramel, the apple just washes it away. There's one less thing for you all to worry about. Glad I can help.

It doesn't matter how old I am. I will always find the name Fatty Doo Doo funny.

Does anyone know where I can find a job as an H.R. Puffnstuff Rep?

(Hurricane joke before it hit.)
The girl on the news said that we're going to start getting the backside of Sandy. Hehe

(After Sandy hit)
Even though we're ok, this whole thing leaves us with such an un-settling, horrible feeling for what happened and what people are going through. It's weird that when this happens, for the next few weeks people are going to be really nice to each other. I can't wait to start hating again. Hopefully by November 6th, I'll feel it.

I went to Shop Rite to get eggs. I used several baskets to avoid putting them all in one.

"hggfjyfss///" - my cat, Spooky, wanted to write on FB. I do like what he had to say.

I realized that I would read more if I ate more fiber.

I saw a woman today working at Dunkin Donuts with a name badge that read Seman. I did not laugh out loud. That would have been rude.

The Garfield comic started in 1981. He's dead by now. That must be old footage we're seeing or a different cat.

I respect anyone who is willing to get help when they see a dog locked in a hot car. However, be careful. The story you are about to hear is true. I saw a dog locked in a car this morning, windows rolled up, at an insurance agency. I called the police. They showed up at the exact moment the perp was coming back to his car. He drew his gun. They drew theirs. "There was a firefight!!"
The dog got out of the car and was furious. Apparently, that dog worked for the Cherry Hill Police Department and was on a stake out to catch a notorious Jewish drug dealer. The "Jewish" isn't a joke. That's a specific detail to establish that I'm not making this

up. Next time, you see a dog in a hot car, don't jump the gun and call for help. Simply give the window two taps. When the dog looks at you, Give him a nod, a wink, a thumbs up, and a "Thank you for doing your part, K9."

Can you do comedy at an online university?

Sometimes I'll dream I'm going to the bathroom and wake up just in time to stop. I worry that my cat might do that when he's in bed with me.

If you attempt to walk across the Grand Canyon on a tightrope, you're an asshole, especially if you have kids. How bad is his marriage?

The unsung heroes are the ones who actually set a tightrope up across the Grand Canyon.

Has anyone ever really walked out of a biker bar, tripped, and knocked over all the bikes in domino formation?

Just putting it out there, Peter Lorre had sex at some point. Imagine what that was like!

"Ba Ba Ba Ba Barbara Ann" - Mike Love

I'm not saying I'm on anything, but I love all my Facebook friends. I would give you all a hug if I could.

Kate Middleton goes into labor around the same time Dennis Farina dies. Coincidence? We're about to find out if reincarnation is real!

The expression "Jeez Louise" was first used in 1923.

I was lying in bed this morning and heard the pre-emptive warning sound that Spooky the cat is about to cough up a hairball, twice. As I decided to search for it, barefoot, in the next room, I learned that sometimes it's clear.

Has anyone copied something from the bible or the torah on silly putty?

Dirty ducks got you down? Dawn Dishwashing Liquid gets grease off your duck with ease.

I have a question for my journalist friends. Is it normal to have as many near death experiences as Lois Lane?

According to a recent poll in my mind, Gotham City has the number one highest crime rate in the world.

I wonder if it was difficult to give ET a noogie.

I am by no means superstitious, but I still don't feel right not saying Knock on Wood at the appropriate times.

Are there any fat guys named Sven?

I'm watching a David Blaine special. If we had to save the earth by sacrificing someone to a volcano, I would have no problem with David Blaine being thrown into it.

Does anyone have footage of David Blaine laughing?

I have a very good friend receiving a colonoscopy today. I want him to know that I'm routing for him. However, even though I can't or won't be there to hold your hand, it does not make me less of a friend.

Is it just me? I always feel dirty when I post some kind of political belief on a social networking site. I totally believe these sites are meant for nonsense and there is no debating that.

Do you think if giants existed they would always be sick because of how high in the atmosphere their heads would be?

I went to sleep with a painful cough so my dreams consisted of vignettes centering around a man experiencing different adventures with a painful cough. Is that indie film material?

This status update is meant to be read in real time.

This status was typed before a live studio audience.

Do you think anyone has 5 cats named, Tootie, Natalie, Blair, Joe, and Geri?

Please share your favorite Neil Diamond saved my life story.

It's been years so for Throwback Thursday "I've been diagnosed with strep throat. The 7th commenter wins a chance to bring me some chicken soup."

These black bear spotting updates in South Jersey are reminiscent of the Andrew Cunanan sightings that were happening in the area in the 90s. Eventually, this bear will take out a famous entrepreneur then off himself.

Word of advice. If there is a line at a self checkout, you don't need your little child playing cashier for you. It's not an important life lesson, unless of course that's your goal for them in life. People are waiting.

I just learned the Mother's Day tradition of eating eggs for breakfast today. It's to represent the mother putting the eggs back into her body to signify the peace and quiet of not having children.

A 70 year old woman today told me she has an old friend who's done comedy for years. I asked her his name and she said I wouldn't know him. He's too old. She said she saw him at the Borgata. I said I might know him.
She said, "No. Different generation." I asked her to tell me his name again and she said no. You won't know him. She told me one more story about him and walked away. Why so shady?

I hope I'm not alone in hating the sentence, "Thank you for supporting live comedy." To me it sounds it seems to make stand-up feel like it's part of a non-profit organization telethon. "As long as the calls keep coming we'll keep giving you round the clock comedy."

Remember folks, It's Earth Day! This is the one day of the year you need to act like you care. Get on the ground and kiss that dirt. Let the earth know you care or it will destroy us all! It's got reps from Whole Foods monitoring your every move. You'll know who they are. They look homeless, but they're not. They also have self-righteous personalities. So for the love of all that is good, recycle today and today only. I'm pretty sure tomorrow we can go back to normal.

Either the neighbor below me is getting tortured by Jigsaw or she's a Dallas fan.

Remember, if you do something good, like give money to the homeless, post it on social media, or else it doesn't count.

The Ashley Madison hack helped my wife and I realize not only that we both love pina coladas, but also getting caught in the rain. This hack really made the marriage stronger.

The moment you think you took your cholesterol meds and realize you took your wife's meth instead... Right??

I could take an adorable picture of the two cats sitting and watching the storm together and write, "My little stormwatchers." It's really a cute scene. Probably the most adorable these two girls have ever looked. There is no question that it would go viral. I'm not going to be that person who keeps posting cat pics, however.

So Pluto jumped on the bandwagon too and claimed he wants to be recognized as a planet again. Good for you, Pluto. Good for you.

From now on, I am to be recognized as tall. You may see me as 5'6, but I'm now 6'1.

July 4

What is everyone getting America today? I need ideas. What do you get for the country that has everything? $2 scratch off tickets? My other dilemma is I don't know where to send the card.

Started the 4th of July off with fireworks! Hopefully, Immodium takes care of that.

Seeing as how my middle name is Wayne, if I were to be a billionaire, I'd have to become Batman. I think the next move should be a Kickstarter campaign to achieve this goal. Now, if you cared about the well being of the world, it's up to you to donate.

I think this is more for the porn stars, themselves, who want to go into space. The fans aren't going to watch for more then several minutes. They can save a lot of time and money if they just wore astronaut suits in that scenario. People would be just as happy.

Next Mother's Day, I'm creating a Build-A-Bear store with an open bar. Anyone want in?

I was just told that the key to looking younger is moisturizer, yoga, and booze. Does anyone want to package this with me and go into business?

As little as I care about anything Bruce Jenner does with his life, I'm happy for him. He did what he needed to in order to be happy and comfortable with himself. He's not hurting anyone.
I've seen a few people on this social media forum here saying that it's immoral and unnatural and there is a special place in hell for

him and these people. Some of the statuses were violent and hateful.

With each negative posting, Christianity was brought into the equation as well.

If you're a good Christian, shouldn't that teach you to be tolerant? Not one of you are perfect and don't have room to criticize anyone else for anything they do with their own life if it has no bearing on you. You're allowed to not like it, it's a free country. If you're spewing this kind of negativity, though, you probably have some of your own issues to work out and you're just projecting it through your hatred of others.

The story you are about to read is true.

Earlier today, I told someone was talking about dumpster diving. I said, I couldn't because or cat litter, dog poop, and old food to say the least.

On my way to the library, about 6pm, I went to the dumpster at my condo community to throw out some trash. When I opened it, there was a treasure trove of what looked to be 20 to 30 porn dvds or more. It wasn't in arms reach, but if I leaned in the side door, I could grab it.

There wasn't alot of trash, but an awful smell. I contemplated, "Do I reach for it? Is there a hidden camera? Is the neighbor who disposed of these watching? How much of a perverted degenerate would I look like, in broad daylight, jumping into a smelly dumpster to gather some porn?"

I decided NO. I don't need it. It's wrong.

I felt like a hero. I ran to the library to return my books. I felt like the sacrifice I made was an automatic conversion to Christianity.

I called my friend, Lindsay, who can be my voice of reason AND is a domestic abuse liason, to brag about my heroic sacrifice. She said, "Are you nuts? Go get it. Who cares?"

Some other friends I reached out to said the same thing. This was already a difficult decision!

I get home. I park and sit in the car wondering how I subtly approach the dumpster and take out piles of dvds.

As I decide to take a last stroll, my neighbor, SISTER Peggy, comes outside to check her mail. I'm on my way to the dumpster with no trash. I had to switch directions and go to the mailbox. "Hi Sister Peggy! Oops. I forgot my mail key!" I already got the mail. I had to go all the way upstairs and get the key to keep the lie legitimate.

Needless to say, the porn is still in the dumpster, much like the briefcase in Fargo.

No matter how good you might be feeling some days, you always feel like you hit rock bottom when you use a port a potty.

I love this quote. "Jason Pollock, you bomb better than anybody I've ever seen." - Chris Alberts

With the water situation as it is on the west coast, is it wrong to waste water with the courtesy flush or is it still acceptable?

If Ken Burns didn't make documentaries, he would probably be hosting an intense Quizzo somewhere.

It's not that I'm not good at trivia, but I still don't see the point in even trying to play Trivial Pursuit with Ken Burns.

My whole life, all I ever wanted was to be a plate spinner on the Ed Sullivan show. Is that too much to ask?

I saw a pastry chef make some amazing Nutella cupcakes today. He followed it with the statement, "If you can think it, you can put it in a cupcake." The possibilities are endless!

I believe that cough syrup is just a placebo.

With the population out of control, we should eliminate all seat belt laws.

Do turkey vultures have any natural predators in NJ? Are we about to become overrun with these monsters?

I wish Morgan Freeman could do narration in my dreams.

If ZZTop's Legs was written in the early part of the 1900s, it would've been called Gams or Stems.

I wonder how many people having dinner with Wallace Shawn ask him to call them Andre.

Nothing weird about putting lamb's blood on my door without having kids. Cats count! I love animals. Happy Pesach!

Elijah must be really hammered by the end of Passover.

I wish Frank Sinatra focused on one geographical location to sing about. Things get confusing.

I'm using a different mug this morning from my norm. Maybe this will create a butterfly effect.

Does exposing only Theresa Caputo as a fraud mean all other mediums are real?

I'm going to start selling hot cakes for extra cash. I hear they sell like...um..

I'm not saying I'm a time traveler, but I knew I was going to type this before I did.

People tell me that if you start to go to the gym every day it becomes a habit. That's bullshit! It never gets easier!

Is there anything in this world more brutal than sitting outdoors at a graduation?

Farts tend to lighten a mood. Try it.

Someone found a baby llama in an alley in Detroit. You won't believe what happened next! Doesn't matter. I'm not going to tell you.

What is a good age to start talking to your pets about sex and is it different with dogs or cats?

Why do people say half dozen when you can just say six? I never understood that.

I'm watching a show. Is anyone going to record the meteor shower tonight?

Winning the 40 million dollar powerball would get me temporarily out of debt.

I've worked with seafood for years, but can never tell when a clam is upsidedown.

Trekkies, help me out. I never recall seeing anyone ever clean up on the Enterprise. Was there ever any dusting done?

Ron Jeremy should star in Fiddler on the Roof.

What is the best vintage for Manischewitz?

People, can you please stop sweating Ebola. You can contract it through sweat.

I believe that employees would be more respectful to customers if the company stopped telling their staff to treat them like family.

Good news! More people in America won the lottery than died of Ebola! So your odds are better of playing the Powerball.

My cat pooped at the same moment my microwave popcorn was ready. I'm unsure how I feel about this combo odor.

Say the word "Blink" a bunch of times. It's a funny word.

Bangor State Fair ad! "They have animals like sea lions and rattlesnakes!" Well, you can't have one without the other.

I just realized that I have a super power. I can make myself pee with my mind.

When "Back to School" supplies hit the store, they never cease to still give me anxiety to this day.

2 MOVIES AND TELEVISION THOUGHTS

I found out a comic friend of mine has an Eddie and the Cruisers credit, but doosn't use it for his intro during a show. I, personally, would be proud of that. Would you?

A friend who just posted, "How am I supposed to do my homework when the Truman Show is on?" Really? If you don't get why that's weird, you need to realize, I'm a movie snob. That is so mundane and random that it's awesome! Wow! "How can I go shopping when there is a Coach marathon on television?"

I just heard a CSI commercial on the radio where they actually said, "You've heard of Mommie Dearest. Well here is Mommie Deadest."

I dare someone to name their son Lando.

I'm catching up on his McMillan and Wife. Does she really die in a plane crash in season 5? Don't tell me! Don't tell me!

My friend, John Kensil talked about Macrame club! What were the first two rules of Macrame club?!

My roomate never heard of To Catch a Predator. When I told him about it, he thought Chris Hansen was one of the Hanson brothers and it confused him.

I'm watching Xanadu and is wondering if the cast is embarrassed if they watch it today.

I just heard What a Feeling by Irene Cara from Flashdance. I feel alive now.

I would like a mechanical owl as a sidekick.

I just put on Snoopy Come Home. I'm going to cry myself to sleep now.

I'm watching Wild Hogs at work. The only way to really watch this movie is to get paid to do it.

There's a leak in the ceiling of part of his room. It's dripping into buckets. I'm sick and cold. I feel like a child from Angela's Ashes.

Superman's real name is Kal-El. My Hebrew name is Mordecchai.

Has anyone ever had a Joe Montegna film festival?

I'm thinking that if we win the Megamillions lottery we could have really special guests at the wedding; like surprise everyone with Wallace Shawn doing a monologue from My Dinner with Andre. Could you think of a better surprise?

If you are hanging out with the dude that 127 Hours is based on and bitch about your day, is he gonna be a dick and remind you of how he lost his arm and drank his own pee? That would get annoying.

For those who are free tonight and have Cinemax, The Hills Have Thighs is on at 10:45. It's the harrowing true story of Sex-starved women holding a man captive in the mountains.

Rick Moranis went to elementary school with Geddy Lee. Hmm. Neat. Just learned that.

I saw a dark cloud outside that resembled Gamera and, for a brief moment, had a glimmer of hope.

Soo... I'm watching Snow White on the Disney Channel. I haven't seen this since the 70s. So the prince heard this girl was dead and decides he has to kiss her corpse? It's a good thing she woke up. That would have been weird. Obviously, she wasn't dead anyway! Dwarves don't know how to check a pulse?

Does anyone else feel that dinner with Matt Dillon would be awk-ward? I can't read that guy.

November 30, 2011
Happy birthday Robert Guillaume!

I'm watching Sigmund the Sea Monster. It's Monday. Anyway, he's in love with a dog and one of the kids just told him that he can't love a dog and "Take a cold shower, if you have to." 70s kid's shows are the best kid's shows!

I'm watching the commentary on Xanadu. Apparently, in the open-ing dance sequence of the movie to the song I'm Alive, they weren't supposed to be glowing. It was radiation poisoning. The director loved it and kept it in.

There is an old Dick Tracy on TCM. The caption read, Dick Tracy is pursuing Fur Pirates. Do I need to say more?

With the Abraham Lincoln, Vampire Hunter popularity, do you think it's time for the George Washington 80s Arcade Owner screenplay my friend, Bob, and I have been tossing around?

What is it about Gavin MacLeod that makes him so watchable?!

I'm watching The Outsiders. Rob Lowe is spooning with C. Thomas Howell. Man or woman, who wouldn't let Rob Lowe spoon them? There's a pretty man right there.

If you really had 101 dalmations in a city apartment, wouldn't you be reported for that?

I'm watching a riveting true story called A Good Day to Die Hard. We could all learn from these movies about the importance of family. The best way for a father and son to truly bond is to take out Russian terrorists together.

The new first rule of Fight Club is Everyone Has To Bring a Dish.

Well, I did not get cast as Christian Grey. I swore that part would have called for an unknown Jon Lovitz type.

Would anyone be surprised if they found out Robert Mitchum was gay? He's just a little too macho.

Think of The Shawshank Redemption narrated by Burl Ives.

I'm sure, like me, many people from my generation had their first exposure to albinos from the film Foul Play.

Does anyone have a copy of an Ed Wynn sex tape?

Are there any actresses today who would be comparable to a modern day Tyne Daly or Sharon Gless?

April 22, 2014
Today is John Waters birthday. I'm so grateful to have discovered his films at such an early age. It really affects the way you watch movies and view the world. If you want to culture your kids, start them young. Make sure they are aware that offbeat is cool.

The performance of Michael Gross in Tremors 5 by far exceeds that of James Franco in 127 Hours. If I give details, there would be spoilers.

I'm watching the Amazing Stories episode, Mirror Mirror. Just an fyi.. only 5 minutes in and a young Sam Waterston is in the bath. You're welcome, Ladies and gentlemen.

Now casting A Miracle Worker on 34th Street. Helen Keller goes to Macy's and proves she's real.

Why, according to Netflix, because I watched Family Guy, does it assume I would like The Passion of the Christ?

Netflix also tells me that because I watched Poltergeist 2, I would like An Officer and a Gentleman.

A gentleman just explained to me this evening that The Wizard of Oz is just a story of two women fighting over a pair of shoes.

3 HORROR

I love horror films. I'm surrounded by so much comedy that to escape I need something dark and disturbing. Though, I'm scared of my own shadow, the thrill of a horror film is that you can experience horrible, twisted things and it's only a movie. When it's over you're safe.

The world needs Troma films. They help you witness the things you'd never dream of and open your mind to a deeper darker place while laughing at it. Troma is healing.

What's the appeal of Twilight? You are not allowed to say that it's because the dudes are hot. Go!

I'm afraid of the boy in the crawl space.

I want to wish all his friends and family, even the Jewish ones, into cartoon land! Fooled you!

I just heard that wild turkeys are attacking cars in Bucks County! It's all happening! Run for the cities!

I encountered the Mexican Goat Sucker this morning!! I'm lucky I got out alive. Stay indoors Cherry Hill!

I'm at the Italian fest. After the alcohol intake, the crowds, and the hot sun, it is turning into a zombie walk.

I'm on a seesaw. I'm stuck in the air and my friend is threatening to get up. I feel like I'm in the movie Saw!

I'm watching little blonde children kill an entire town with their eyes. Superman seems powerless against them. #village-ofthedamned

I'm watching Thinner. It's hard to take the evil gypsy seriously after seeing him as the father in My Big Fat Greek Wedding.

I'm watching The Birds on Cinemax. I'm a little disappointed that Alfred Hitchcock didn't have a scene where Suzanne Pleshette and Tippi Hedren kiss.

I finally solved a Rubik's Cube, but it released the damn Cenobytes! Well, take the good with the bad. At least I figured it out.

I just heard the legend of the 9-fingered nun of Riverside! I am frightened.

I think it's been a while since I've worried about the blob issue. Hopefully, it's a cold winter so that thing stays frozen in the north pole. That is the biggest concern with global warming.

Pinhead vs Beetlejuice! Who would win?

Would be a bad omen to be stuck in the middle of John Lithgow and William Shatner on a plane?

I changed it over to Predators. A little more interesting than the Owls of Ga'Hoole. Owls are cute, but dull conversationalists.

Don't trust potatoes! Something went wrong!

I think it would be really neat to see a scene in a movie where you think something horrible is about to happen to a person walking around a house alone, but a cat jumps out instead!

Which is a more obscure name, Sigourney or Ripley?

If Invasion of the Body Snatchers happened, I'd just go with it. It's really a great way to turn your mind off.

I want to make a third Ring movie where the ghost girl comes back and has to transfer videos to dvd

I just joined a gym called The Silent Hill Fitness Center. It's a little weird in there, but it really forces cardio.

So were they able to change the channel in Poltergeist?
Or was it stuck on The Other Side network?

I just watched The Purge. If this existed, would they cancel comedy shows for that night?

Ain't no Halloween party like a Debbie Boone Halloween party, cause a Debbie Boone Halloween party don't stop.

Watching Monkey Shines makes me fear my cats. All of a sudden they're becoming very smart.

The Hunchback of Notre Dame or Igor could never have been a detective because of the play on words people would tease him with every time he said, "I have a hunch about something."

Jaws was the first horror film I ever saw. It was in the 70s and I still don't like to swim in the ocean. Thanks Jurassic Park movies, now I'm afraid to hike on dinosaur infested islands.

Who's up for going as a Human Centipede for Halloween?

How annoying would it have been to be the neighbor of Linda Blair's character's family in The Exorcist?

Alot of people ask what a romantic night in with Jason and Laura entails. The answer is a David Cronenberg marathon with burritos.

Seeing as how Easter Sunday is approaching I was discussing the movie Reanimator with a female friend who has never seen the film. The famous disembodied head being held by the headless body between the woman's legs scene came up. She asked, quite adamantly, if the woman was pissed when the hero burst in to save her because she never got to "finish." She missed the point that this is supposed to be a scary thing, but I feel this is good insight into where certain female priorities lie.

"Killing me won't bring your apples back!" - The Wicker Man #I don't think I'll ever have a need to say that.

The lesson I get from True Blood is that it's not easy to be a vampire. I guess my problems are not very significant compared to the undead.

Since Max Brooks wrote World War Z, it would've made it so much better to have had Mel Brooks direct it.

Who is a more depressing filmmaker? Lars Von Trier or Zapruder?

There are some times in my life when I see movies coming to theaters soon that I'm so grateful for the existence of Troma.

4 THANKSGIVING

Here's a new idea for a Thanksgiving drinking game. I want to do a shot after every mass text.

I love Thanksgiving! I just ate a banana. My stomach is like, "That's it?" He has no idea. Haha! I'm like, "Just wait, pal." This is the calm before the storm.

I was really looking forward to surprising my stomach with the dinner tonight. Now my stomach is pissed and he's turning on me.

To us, this is a holiday weekend. Household appliances don't share that knowledge. A kitchen sink, for example, might decide to spring a leak underneath without any knowledge of what may or may not have been many years ago. It's just an ordinary day for Mr. Sink.

Remember.. Don't wish anyone a Happy Thanksgiving yet unless you know for sure that you won't be talking to them till after the holiday. It just makes it awkward if you encounter them again.

Can you guys stop acting like heroes for not shopping on Thanksgiving? Why is this, suddenly, a huge deal? The employees usually get time and a half. The economy is stimulated. What about the ones who aren't celebrating the holiday? Now they have a place to go!
If none of us go out, the ones working will be pretty damn bored. I hope nobody does that traditional going out to the movies on Thanksgiving! Don't get gas either! Seriously, you're not a hero just because YOU can take a day off from shopping. I don't mean to rant, but it's so annoying when people act like heroes in their own head one day of the year and an asshole the rest. Sorry. This was all spurned from a conversation I overheard at the bank

where this woman was acting like an outspoken saint because she said if the banks were open she wouldn't go there.

Happy Thanksgiving to all my friends and family.. That being said.. This is a warning. Invasion of the Body Snatchers may be upon us! Whatover you do tonight, don't go to sleep!! That's how they get you!

Please finish this sentence in quotations... I just saw a porn star on Twitter use this phrase to promote her website. "If you are lonely, bored or feel like masturbating during #Thanksgiving, don't forget....

5 CHRISTMAS

Christmas is my other favorite time of year besides Halloween. I love the music and the festiveness you feel apart from the anger and frustration of the people getting unnecessarily impatient trying to create that perfect Christmas. Partially, because I witness this first hand working in retail and I go home to a peaceful house with my wife and cats. Christmas is a time when I feel blessed not having children.

Do you prefer We are the World or Do they know it's Christmas? American or English?

Looks like there is snow in Africa this Christmas time. Should we thank Bob Geldof?

I just heard a guy on the radio talk about a man with the biggest, magic sack there ever was. I don't know what to think.

"Christmas comes this time each year." Very provocative line from the Beach Boys Little St. Nick. Brilliant.

This is sort of stolen from a friend's status, BUT, if you're dealing with anyone in retail this weekend, be nice to them. Imagine how you'd feel if you were dealing with that shit this holiday season.

(Really, this is for Rosh Hashana)
Happy new year! Anyone staying up to watch the dreidel drop?

"We won't come until we get some." is a line in what Christmas song?

I just heard the song "It's the Most Wonderful Time of the Year." They mention scary ghost stories. Is this a time of year to share those? I have been missing out!

Christmas shopping on Vicodin opens up your world! You know what? For some reason, I feel like Laura would need tractor tires.

Brenda Lee could be an adverb.

I'm waiting for the dentist. Apparently, he used to work for Santa as an elf. They actually made a made for tv movie on his life.

As a Jew, I would like someone to tell me when the Christmas diarrhea ends. I'm not familiar with this part of your tradition, goyams and shiksas.

There is a very annoying whiney kid in front of me in line actually telling this clerk that his mom is dying and he needs to get her these special shoes for Christmas, but doesn't have money. Join the club. I don't even know how he got here. I'm about to get security.

I think it would be kind of fun to build a snowman and pretend he's Parson Brown! People would find that hilarious.

Burl Ives singing Lavender Blue would never go over if it came out today. Come to think of it, I don't even understand it from back then. Maybe somebody will remix that song.

Thanks Kegan for recommending the Christmas classic, The Big Bad Wolf of Wall Street, to show my 10 year old niece and 6 year old nephew. We're starting in 2 minutes! I hope the sing a longs are as good as you say.

I got to perform at a benefit for the Mummers last night. Sometimes I forget that people not from the Philly/South Jersey area don't know what Mummers are. They are South Philly tough guys dressed in the most flamboyant costumes and march through the streets on New Year's Day.

I'm really hoping 2010 will be a great year. Anything should be better than 2009. Let's get on it and help each other have great life changes this year. Just like Bill & Ted had a song that changed the entire universe, let this be the status update that is comparable to the Bill & Ted song.

Happy new year! Someone said the possibilities are limitless. That's not always a positive thing. Some of you will have an amazing year! For some others, however, it's going to be the worst year of your life. There is really no way of knowing any of this. Just enjoy it while you can. I just hope it doesn't start tomorrow for you. That would suck.

Do you feel New Year's Resolutions are considered hack material by now in the comedy world of life? Waiting till the new year for a life change is an excuse to procrastinate. If you start in the new year, chances are you're bored by February. Just make a life change when you're ready or when the doctor tells you. I conclude with a dammit.

6 LAURA

There's an old joke that works when people see Laura and I to-gether. "He's either got a big dick or a lot of money." In my case, however, she's got low self-esteem and that works for me.
My wife is stunning and has the most perfect personality.
I've known this woman for 15 years before we started getting to really know each other. It's true it happens when you're not looking all thanks to a physical pain I suffered and mentioned on Face-book, which I'll bring up in a moment.
There is something she said to me that really stuck, "I don't go for people for their looks. I am interested in their soul." That doesn't do much for my self-esteem physically, but I'll take it. Sometimes there is no rhyme or reason for why things happen, but she puts up with me and that's fine.

We became Facebook friends in the beginning of summer 2010. This is the status below I posted that made her laugh to the point where she wanted to get to know me better.
Things haven't changed either. Me being in physical pain or just being uncomfortable, never fails to amuse her to the fullest extent.

Jason Pollock
August 31, 2010 ·

My whole day was thrown into upheaval when I bit into a mat-zoh and it stabbed my gums and just about knocked a tooth out. The matzoh is still there!

A FEW OTHER SOCIAL MEDIA QUIPS REGARDING MY LOVE LIFE

Love is not counted on dollars spent. Right people?

45

Dan Fogelberg might be dead, but I have the best girl in the world in my life! See. What does this show you?

Laura loves the sound of vanilla.

When 2 people live in a one bedroom apartment, it's a bad idea for both parties to take a laxative at the same time.

Laura just said to me out of nowhere, "I'm looking at you, but I'm thinking of potato salad." What would Freud say?

Laura is talking about work in her sleep. She should get paid over time for being there in her dreams.

As I was sitting on the bed describing my new workout plan to Laura, the bed collapsed underneath me. I think I'm better at comedy when it's not planned out.

Laura was questioning how I know that is not an old wasp's nest on the deck. She, obviously, doesn't know that new hive smell.

Just to give an idea of what kind of horror connoisseur my beautiful wife is, she referred to the Texas Chainsaw Massacre as The Chain Man of Alcatraz. She couldn't figure out how I didn't know what she meant, loving horror movies and all. I just thought I'd share.

Regarding Cirque Du Soleil, Laura said, "I thought it was just men with painted penises." I couldn't not share that.

I'm trying to convince my wife it's ok to fly, eventually. If some air tragedy happens any where in the world, could we not report it within earshot of wherever she might see it? Tell every single person please. Let's just keep this quiet.

I never thought I'd get married. It's wonderful having a woman you can touch whenever you want AND it's completely legal. To have a conversation about history while grabbing a butt cheek is what marriage is all about.

As Dark Side of the Moon correlates perfectly with the Wizard of Oz, if you start playing The Wall at 2 days before your wedding, it also blends perfectly.

I'm inventing a time machine and getting married in 1980. We are registering at Two Guys and having the reception at The Ground Round.

I'm thinking Ferns for the centerpieces at the wedding.

Happy two year Anniversary Laura Podolak-Pollock! I'm supposed to write something like, "Two years ago I married my best friend.. blah blah blah." I just can't. Since we've been together, there's been a brain injury, deaths, strange natural disasters, appliances have broken, and awful debts. Being with you, however, makes all that seem somewhat tolerable. I love you!

On their anniversaries, I see a lot of, "On .... years ago today. I married my best friend.. and the best choice I ever made... blah blah blah.. "
Laura Podolak-Pollock, three years ago today we got married. You don't remember anyone from the wedding and we barely remember the actual wedding itself. The fact that we both forget our anniversary every year and are happy and supportive of each other every day means we're doing great. I love that you hate Valentine's Day and all the other holidays that mean nothing. I know I

picked the right one. I love you! Public mush is kind of lame, but I had to do something. I still can't believe I'm married!

Laura told me that she would've overslept the other morning if I didn't tap her and say, "Laura, wake up. Your alarm is going off." I didn't. I was making coffee. At what age does dementia start to set in?

She actually woke me up in the middle of a deep sleep by shouting out loud at 2am, "I wonder if a monkey on a motorcycle has the same fears as a human."

7 LIFE AND DEATH

People tell me to live life as if you're going to die tomorrow. I live like I'm going to die any second. That tends to make me a bit anxious. I'm trying to change, but it's difficult. I was watching Frosty the Snowman and thinking, "Here's a man who is always happy and he could die at room temperature!"
I wish I could adopt that attitude. I used to say that I have an irrational fear of death. As I think about it, I think it's pretty rational. No matter how good this book might or might not be, at least I left something behind. God, I hope this isn't it. ;)

I want to know if it's possible to live in the moment and obsess about the future at the same time, because I feel I do.

(This is actually something my grandmother said at a seafood restaurant to the hostess while dementia was taking over. Sad, but you have to laugh.)
We're just innocent people looking to have some fish.

(Rule of Three a few years ago)
Gary Coleman, Dennis Hopper, and Art Linkletter. That's three. OR are we not counting Art Linkletter because most people thought he was already dead for years.

My last status update will read, "Jason Pollock should not be Facebooking while he's dri...."

I'm glad I don't remember my briss.

When your day starts out like it's one of the best mornings of your life, you need to remember it can only get worse from there.

What is the etiquette if you are walking with someone and you really have to pee, bad, but before you get to the bathroom that person has a heart attack. Can you go pee and be right back or call 911 on your way?

Remember whenever your stressing out about anything in life, one day we can all be wiped out by an asteroid and none of it will matter, so enjoy life while you can.

I wonder if a big fat guy ever got lodged in the walk-through heart at the Franklin Institute and had a heart attack. That would be ironic. That's exactly how I want to go.

(*Proudest moment - This status is more exciting than the actual story.*)
Were you wondering if I saved a baby goat today? Because I DID!

Morning news in Bar Harbor, Maine on NBC, "Portland, Maine is awaiting results on the First homocide of the year..." Imagine if we didn't have a homocide till August in the tri-state area?!

Day 2; Monday: I still feel the sickness alive and well inside my body. The head pain, the scratchy throat, the runny nose. Oh how the nose runs. The germs seem to have stabilized. Though, it has not gotten worse, the situation has not improved. I fear as though I will be unconscious soon as for the AlkaSeltzer Night will take affect. If I survive till the morrow, I might need the powerful antibiotics. Time will tell. Godspeed.

Goodnight everyone and remember; That which does not kill me is usually not life threatening.

Do you ever feel like your whole life is a lot of, "Oh yeah. I gotta do that."?

Elvis died at 42. It's weird to think that at 40 years old, this is what's known as his later years!

If I say, "I'm going to the bathroom one last time." It's not forever. It just means before I leave.

No matter what troubles you have or what's going on in the world, the power of Neil Diamond will make everything alright.

When I got in my car to leave work, Islands in the Stream was on the radio. Something came over me and I couldn't bring myself to turn it off. Day four of the new anti-depression meds.

No matter what horrors are going on in the world; whether it's violent acts of terror or frightening weather phenomenon brought on by global warming, none of it matters when I'm home and cozy and realize that I have to freaking get dressed and go to the store for milk for the morning!!

Someone mentioned that they heard short people live longer than tall people. I need to know when and which tall people please.

I always found it interesting that at Jewish funerals we watch the body lowered into the ground and everyone takes turns with the shovel pouring dirt onto the casket. It's a very positive event. Apparently, the reason we do this is if we do a little bit of filling in the grave first, we get a discount.

I'm thinking that you never know what your last status update will be. So people, write each update as if it's your last.

ABOUT THE AUTHOR

Jason Pollock is a comedian/actor/booker and catering driver at a specialty food store. Now he's a self-published author. Sorry ladies, he's married. It wouldn't matter anyway. He's terrible with money. The metabolism is slowing down. He's lazy. You're not missing out on this guy. But he thanks you for reading.

49862111R00038

Made in the USA
Charleston, SC
08 December 2015